# Let's hold tight our steering

*Keeping the AI still in the copilot seat*

# Table of Contents

## Introduction: The AI Copilot Philosophy

For someone like me, who likes exploring technologies, who (for a lucky coincidence) was born with a PC at home in the 1980s, and who is genuinely interested in learning, the day when I tested Chat GPT was love at first sight.

Can you imagine an overwhelming feeling like someone is gifting you an all-you-can-eat ticket to a candy shop, and you do not know where to start?

Well, on that day, although sceptical, I prompted the first question (the one that usually everyone statistics say is asked by dummy first users), *"How can I make money?"* and something magic happened. A meaningful, although quite obvious, answer: *"You should find a job, invest..."* started being printed in front of my eyes, giving me the impression that the computer was interacting with me like never before.

My genuine curiosity pushed me to test the tool to its limits, and since the beginning, I could identify some hallucinations, like fake references generated or the recurring use of specific words; at that time, it was so annoying, but now, indeed, most of these buzzwords are very popular for those who "delve into" (LOL) these systems.

I started considering Chat GPT as my best friend, complaining, thanking, challenging… However, I realised that the message *"Ask anything"* was (partially) true, but it was always waiting for my essential input.

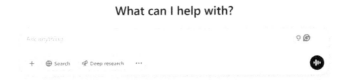

Almost immediately, I figured out that if the answer was not correct, most of the time, it was my fault for not being able to craft a proper request. However, after a lot of self-training, despite the continuous new models released, I still had some doubts about the answers.

My main question was: *"Am I sure the system has been trained enough?"*. Wondering about that, I instantly identified the first limitation of these systems: **we do not know how they have been trained and which document fed them**.

The solution was handy anyway: **buying the subscriptions allowed me to upload documents to train the model myself!**

When I still hear people complaining about the proficiency of the systems, I already know that, in 99% of the cases, they:

- did not buy the subscription,
- do not know how to prompt or
- ask questions about which model was not pre-trained.

I've heard friends who consider Chat GPT a lady, a man, or a robot. Indeed, it is now an essential part of our lives.

It is accelerating many tasks, like before technologies like the PC itself, the mobile phone or others, in the past, helped us to facilitate something. Despite the fear from some that it will let jobs disappear, I am very convinced that the models will definitely replace some jobs, especially those that rely on routine (e.g.

secretarial, admin and similar. I want to add: finally!), but they can save us a lot of time to dedicate to other strategic tasks. Ultimately, we are still the drivers.

Let us look back at some technologies that were deployed in the past and generated controversies and fear of job losses, and let us consider the analogies.

- Does the phone start calling itself?
- Does the calculator create the equations?
- Does the car (even those ready for autonomous driving) know where to go independently?

Likewise, AI does not operate independently; it requires our direction, refinement, and validation. The key is understanding that these systems are tools, not replacements for critical thinking or strategic decision-making.

Same here; Chat GPT and similar systems are still waiting for us to "*Ask anything*". Furthermore, behind this question, the developers hope that the transformer won't be tricked into harm, that it received enough training, and that it will not start creating nonsense.

I believe, in this case, we can still take the driver's seat and ask GPT to be our copilot. However, to be on the safest side, I also still prefer to feed the copilot with the right maps to avoid hitting the wall.

If we truly intend to benefit from AI as a copilot, we must engage with it actively, refine our inputs, verify outputs, and, when necessary, provide it with better data to work with. We will, therefore, ensure that AI serves as a reliable assistant rather than a blind guide. Ultimately, the quality of its contributions depends on the quality of our interactions with it—reinforcing the principle that, no matter how advanced AI becomes, human oversight remains essential.

*Abu Dhabi, 05.03.2025*

*Dr Alessio Faccia*

# Chapter 1: The Art of Asking – Prompting Beyond the Surface

## Understanding the role of probability in AI outputs

Artificial Intelligence models, particularly Generative AI like GPT, operate through probability rather than deterministic logic. These systems do not "understand" language in a human sense but instead, predict and generate text based on statistical associations learned during training. This probabilistic nature of AI leads to both its strengths and limitations.

### Step-by-Step Mechanism of Generative AI

1. **Tokenisation of Input.** When a user inputs text into an AI model, the first step involves breaking the text into **tokens**. These are not always whole words; instead, they are fragments that the model has been trained on (e.g., "playing" might be split into "play" and "ing").

2. **Vector Representation and Context Encoding.** Each token is converted into a numerical vector using an **embedding model**, which places similar words in a high-dimensional space based on contextual meaning.

3. **Attention Mechanism (Transformers)**
   - AI models like GPT use **self-attention mechanisms** (from the Transformer architecture) to determine the relevance of each word in the input sequence relative to others.
   - It allows the model to retain context over long passages, making it more coherent.

4. **Probability Distribution Generation**
   - For each token generated, the model **calculates the probability** of every possible next token based on previous tokens.
   - This probability distribution is derived from the massive dataset used during training.

- The AI then samples from this distribution, often using a method such as **temperature scaling** or **top-k sampling** to control randomness.

5. **Text Generation Through Probabilistic Selection**
   - The AI does not "decide" on words in a deterministic way but **selects** the most probable next word based on learned patterns.
   - It explains why different runs of the same prompt can generate different responses—**it is not recalling information but predicting based on probabilities**.

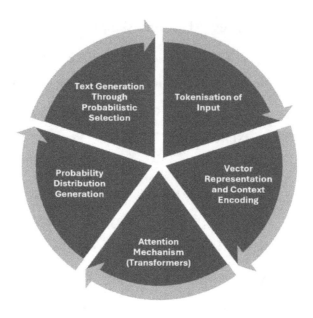

## Why AI Is Exposed to the Chinese Room Argument

The so-called "Chinese Room argument" (proposed by John Searle) questions whether an AI that manipulates symbols truly "understands" language. AI models process and generate text purely based on probability and learned correlations—they do not possess comprehension or reasoning:

- *AI predicts rather than thinks*. Its responses emerge from probabilities of words appearing together in training data, not from true knowledge.

- *AI lacks grounded semantics.* It does not comprehend the meaning behind concepts but mimics structure.
- *AI cannot internally verify the truth.* It does not reason or verify logical consistency unless explicitly trained with factual correction mechanisms.

For instance, an AI might generate a plausible-sounding but incorrect medical diagnosis because it associates symptoms with certain terms rather than understanding the actual cause-and-effect relationships of diseases.

## Impact of Incorrect Training Data on AI Responses

Since AI learns patterns from data rather than meaning, the accuracy of outputs depends heavily on the quality and balance of training datasets.

*Probability Amplifies Training Biases*

If AI is trained on many incorrect documents and few correct ones, it assigns higher probabilities to incorrect associations. For example, if 70% of documents state that "the sun orbits the Earth" and only 30% state the reverse, the AI might wrongly consider the incorrect fact more likely.

*Hallucination Risks Increase with Poor Data*

AI generates responses even when unsure because <u>it always selects a probable answer rather than admitting ignorance</u>. If misleading information is overrepresented in training data, AI confidently generates plausible but incorrect statements.

## Reinforcement of Common Myths and Misconceptions

Since AI models optimise for fluency rather than accuracy, common misconceptions (e.g., "humans use only 10% of their brains") may be repeated if they appear frequently in training data.

## AI as a Probabilistic, Not Deterministic, System

- ➢ AI models predict rather than understand.
- ➢ Outputs are generated probabilistically, meaning they reflect training patterns rather than verified truths.
- ➢ The quality of responses depends on the quality of data—if trained poorly, AI models will amplify errors probabilistically.
- ➢ AI is exposed to the Chinese Room problem, meaning it manipulates symbols but does not genuinely comprehend them.

## Tokens

Tokens are the fundamental building blocks of AI-generated text. They do not always correspond to full words but can be words, parts of words, or even individual characters, depending on how the AI model has been trained to process language. When a user inputs a prompt, the model does not interpret it as a sentence in the way a human would. Instead, it tokenises the text, converting it into a sequence of numerical representations.

For example, the phrase "Artificial Intelligence is powerful." might be broken down into separate tokens such as:

- "Artificial,"
- "Intelligence,"
- "is," and
- "powerful."

Each of these tokens is then processed based on probabilities learned from the model's training data. Below is a tokens' breakdown.

Tokens    Characters
166       675

```
{
"messages": [
{"role": "system", "content": "You are a personal assistant called Jetch
atAI.
You will answer questions about the speakers and sessions at the droidcon
SF conference.
The conference is on June 8th and 9th, 2023 on the UCSF campus in Mission
Bay.It starts at 8am and finishes by 6pm.
Your answers will be short and concise, since they will be required to
fit on a mobile device display.
When showing session information, always include the subject, speaker,
location, and time.
ONLY show the description when responding about a single session. Only
use the functions you have been provided with."},
{"role": "user", "content": "what sessions are on now?"},
]
```

Source: https://devblogs.microsoft.com/surface-duo/android-openai-chatgpt-15/

The number of tokens in a response influences how AI generates text, but it does not determine accuracy. Models like GPT function by predicting the most likely next token based on the previous ones rather than retrieving pre-existing, verified knowledge. It means that increasing the number of tokens in a prompt or response does not inherently improve correctness. Instead, it merely extends the probabilistic process, increasing the likelihood of irrelevant, redundant, or even incorrect outputs. Long responses also introduce the risk of exceeding the model's context window, which is the limit on how much past information the AI can consider at any given time. If the input or generated text is too lengthy, the model starts to lose earlier details, which can lead to contradictions or a loss of coherence.

Using tokens efficiently rather than excessively is essential when prompting AI. A well-structured, precise question will guide the model to focus on the relevant aspects, whereas an overly verbose prompt may dilute its attention and introduce unnecessary complexity. For example, asking, *"Explain how neural networks process input step by step, focusing on weight updates and backpropagation."* is more effective than *"Can you tell me, in detail, how a neural network works in AI and how it processes information step by step?"* The second version, despite using more tokens, does not necessarily lead to a better response. <u>It is not the length but the clarity of the prompt that enhances AI performance.</u>

Prompt engineering alone is insufficient to guarantee accurate or meaningful responses because AI operates on a probabilistic basis rather than true comprehension. The model predicts the most statistically likely sequence of words based on its training data, but it does not verify information for accuracy. If the training data contains a high volume of incorrect or misleading documents, the model will tend to reinforce those errors, even when given a well-phrased prompt. It highlights the importance of proper pre-training with original, high-quality data. AI cannot differentiate between truth and widely repeated falsehoods unless explicitly corrected through training.

One of the greatest risks of AI's probabilistic nature is the "**herd effect,**" where frequently repeated but incorrect information dominates the model's responses simply because it appears more often in the training data. AI does not assess credibility but rather statistical occurrence. If misinformation is widely spread, AI is more likely to reinforce it, making it unreliable unless supplemented by external verification. It is particularly dangerous in fields such as law, medicine, and finance, where factual precision is crucial. Without external expertise, AI-generated responses may appear fluent and well-structured but still contain fundamental inaccuracies.

Expert knowledge remains essential in AI-assisted work because only a domain specialist can critically evaluate AI outputs and identify potential errors. AI cannot independently validate whether its generated response is correct; it can only generate what seems most statistically likely based on prior patterns. This limitation means that human oversight is necessary to distinguish between accurate and misleading results. Users must not only craft effective prompts but also possess the expertise to assess and refine the information provided by AI. The reliability of AI depends not only on how well it is prompted but also on the quality of its training data and the ability of users to filter its outputs with a critical eye.

Most of the time, when GPT produces poor results, the issue is not with the AI itself but with how it is being used. Many users assume that simply asking a question will yield an expert-level answer, yet they fail to refine their prompts or structure them effectively. Advanced AI models require clear, precise, and well-structured inputs to generate meaningful responses. Those who lack skill in prompting often receive vague or incorrect outputs, not because the AI is incapable but because they have not given it the necessary context or direction.

Additionally, the version of the AI being used is a discriminating factor. Free-tier models are significantly less capable than their advanced counterparts, lacking the depth, accuracy, and updated datasets that premium versions offer. Users relying on these basic models and expecting high-level responses are bound to be disappointed. A skilled user working with an advanced AI version can achieve far superior results compared to an untrained user using an outdated or limited model. The difference is not just in the AI but in how well the human interacts with it.

**Connecting different knowledge domains for more reliable AI results**

AI models operate probabilistically, generating responses based on statistical relationships within their training data rather than genuine comprehension. This inherent limitation means that outputs can be contextually relevant but factually incomplete or incorrect if the model lacks exposure to the full spectrum of knowledge necessary for a given inquiry. The reliability of AI-generated results significantly improves when different knowledge domains are integrated, as this reduces the risk of domain-specific biases, knowledge gaps, and overfitting to a single field's heuristics.

Multidisciplinarity is essential in enhancing AI reasoning and response accuracy. When a prompter incorporates cross-domain knowledge, the AI can generate more comprehensive and contextually valid outputs by drawing on patterns from multiple fields rather than reinforcing isolated assumptions within a single domain.

For example, financial risk assessment benefits from insights not only from economics and accounting but also from behavioural psychology, cybersecurity, and regulatory compliance. Without this interconnected approach, AI may provide mechanistically correct yet practically flawed outputs due to a lack of domain intersection.

The knowledge of the prompter is equally critical, as AI does not autonomously prioritise the most relevant connections between fields. <u>A user with expertise in multiple domains can structure queries in a way that forces the AI to consider broader perspectives, mitigating the risks of one-dimensional answers</u>. It is particularly relevant when dealing with probabilistic models, where the absence of explicit connections in the training set can lead to isolated reasoning. An informed prompter strategically designs prompts that encourage AI to cross-reference information, aligning its outputs with real-world complexity rather than theoretical abstraction. Without this level of prompt engineering, AI remains constrained to surface-level pattern matching, reinforcing existing biases rather than synthesising new, reliable knowledge.

## Chapter 2: Hallucinations and Noise – Separating Fact from Fiction

## How AI Generates Hallucinations and Why They Persist

AI-generated hallucinations occur when the model produces content that is either factually incorrect, logically inconsistent, or entirely fabricated. These errors stem from the probabilistic nature of generative AI, which does not retrieve facts but instead predicts the most statistically likely next word based on prior training data. Since AI models are trained on vast datasets containing both reliable and unreliable sources, they sometimes create responses that appear coherent yet lack factual accuracy.

The underlying issue lies in how AI fills gaps in knowledge. When a model encounters a prompt that lacks a direct match in its training data, it does not acknowledge uncertainty but instead extrapolates a plausible answer. This process can generate convincing but false information, including nonexistent references, fabricated historical events, or incorrect numerical data. Hallucinations persist because the model does not possess a verification mechanism—it assigns confidence to its outputs based purely on linguistic probability, not empirical validation. Additionally, AI models are susceptible to reinforcing errors, especially when trained on sources that frequently repeat misconceptions or include biased interpretations of facts.

Hallucinations also become more prevalent when AI is prompted with highly specific, obscure, or poorly structured queries. If the dataset does not contain sufficient corroborating evidence for a particular claim, the AI compensates by inventing details that fit the statistical patterns it has learned. It makes it particularly dangerous in professional fields such as medicine, law, and finance, where precision is essential. The absence of a ground truth within the model means that, unless external verification is applied, hallucinated responses can propagate misinformation with deceptive confidence.

## Techniques to Verify AI-Generated Content

Since AI does not inherently validate its outputs, users must implement systematic verification techniques to ensure the reliability of AI-generated information. One effective method is fact-checking through primary sources. Rather than accepting AI responses at face value, users should cross-check factual statements against official records, peer-reviewed research, regulatory databases, and established industry guidelines. AI can summarise existing knowledge efficiently, but it cannot differentiate between verified and unverified data unless explicitly fine-tuned for such a function.

Another essential technique is **reverse querying**, where users reformulate their prompts to test the consistency of AI-generated claims. When slightly altering the wording of a question or requesting multiple versions of an answer, inconsistencies in responses can reveal potential hallucinations. If an AI model provides different answers to variations of the same question, this signals a lack of stable reference points in its training data.

In cases where numerical data is involved, performing external calculations and benchmarking results against authoritative financial reports, scientific papers, or government datasets is crucial. AI models frequently misinterpret or fabricate numerical figures due to their inability to perform real-time calculations or maintain absolute numerical precision. Users relying on AI for quantitative analysis should validate outputs using domain-specific tools such as Bloomberg for financial data, PubMed for medical research, or LexisNexis for legal references.

Another verification method is to trace the logical structure of AI-generated content. Many hallucinations arise from AI's reliance on linguistic coherence rather than factual integrity. Evaluating whether an answer follows logical causality, aligns with existing knowledge frameworks, and maintains internal consistency can help distinguish between authentic insights and artificially constructed statements.

# The Importance of Cross-Referencing with Credible Sources

The most effective safeguard against AI-generated misinformation is cross-referencing with established, authoritative sources (and your own knowledge, if possible!). AI models do not have an intrinsic reliability filter; they are only as accurate as the data they were trained on. Without external validation, users risk accepting synthetically generated but factually incorrect outputs as truth. In fields where misinformation can have serious consequences—such as legal judgments, financial investment decisions, or medical diagnoses—depending solely on AI without independent verification is highly dangerous.

Cross-referencing should involve evaluating multiple sources across different domains to confirm factual accuracy. Using high-impact academic journals, government publications, regulatory filings, and industry reports helps counteract AI's tendency to favour probabilistically common but potentially false information. Additionally, consulting experts in the field allows users to detect subtle but significant errors that AI might overlook, particularly in highly technical disciplines where domain-specific nuances are essential.

AI's ability to generate fluent and persuasive text can make hallucinations harder to detect, especially for non-experts who might lack the background knowledge to critically assess AI-generated statements. It makes it even more critical to integrate independent validation processes into AI-driven workflows. As AI adoption increases across industries, the responsibility of ensuring factual integrity and knowledge reliability remains firmly on the user. AI should be treated as an advanced assistive tool, not a standalone source of truth.

# Chapter 3: The Knowledge Paradox – AI and Intellectual Decline

## How Over-Reliance on AI Can Lower Human Cognitive Skills

The increasing dependence on AI for information processing and decision-making presents a paradox: while these models enhance efficiency, they also risk diminishing human cognitive abilities. AI models like GPT, with their capacity to generate coherent and contextually relevant responses within seconds, create an illusion of effortless knowledge acquisition. However, when individuals consistently turn to AI instead of engaging in critical analysis, independent problem-solving, or deep learning, they progressively weaken their cognitive reflexes, particularly in areas such as logical reasoning, information synthesis, and problem formulation.

Human cognition thrives on the process of active engagement, where knowledge is constructed through inquiry, analysis, and contextual understanding. AI, by contrast, operates through probabilistic text generation, presenting conclusions without the intermediate steps that would otherwise reinforce memory retention and deeper comprehension. Studies in cognitive psychology suggest that passive consumption of pre-generated answers reduces long-term knowledge retention and adaptive reasoning. Without regular intellectual challenges, individuals may experience a decline in analytical depth as they become accustomed to deferring complex thought processes to AI systems rather than actively engaging with information.

Another critical risk emerges in domains where expert intuition and tacit knowledge are fundamental. AI can simulate expertise but lacks experiential learning—the intuitive grasp of patterns, exceptions, and contextual nuances developed through years of exposure to a discipline. Over-reliance on AI, in such cases, substitutes lived experience with pattern-matching heuristics, leading to potential degradation of professional judgment. Suppose AI becomes the default tool for decision-making. In that case, users may lose the ability to assess their outputs critically, assuming correctness based on fluency rather than verifying through domain-specific logic.

## The Danger of Outsourcing Thinking

AI's ability to provide instant, well-structured responses fosters a passive mode of engagement, where users shift from active problem-solvers to passive recipients of AI-generated content. This reliance on automated reasoning mechanisms reduces the necessity for cognitive struggle, which is essential for intellectual development. The process of forming hypotheses, testing assumptions, and refining arguments is fundamental to knowledge acquisition, yet AI tempts users to bypass these steps entirely, delivering polished conclusions without requiring effort.

One of the most serious consequences of outsourcing thinking to AI is the gradual erosion of epistemic vigilance—the human ability to evaluate information sources critically. Traditionally, individuals have developed mechanisms to assess credibility based on source reliability, argument coherence, and evidential support. AI disrupts this process by generating text that appears authoritative, regardless of whether it is factually correct. This effect is particularly dangerous in fields such as academia, journalism, and law, where the integrity of conclusions depends on rigorous evidence-based reasoning.

The risk intensifies in professional environments where AI systems are integrated into decision-making frameworks. When AI-generated recommendations are treated as authoritative without independent verification, professionals may begin to trust outputs unquestioningly, reducing their role to that of validators rather than critical analysts. This shift can create a self-reinforcing feedback loop, where AI-generated knowledge replaces human expertise, weakening the foundational skills that industries and intellectual disciplines rely on.

## Practical Strategies to Maintain Intellectual Independence

To counteract the risk of cognitive decline due to AI reliance, individuals must adopt strategies that ensure active engagement with knowledge rather than passive consumption. One approach is structured interaction with AI, where users treat AI not as an oracle but as a tool for augmentation rather than substitution. It means actively questioning AI-generated responses, seeking alternative perspectives, and challenging assumptions instead of accepting them at face value.

Maintaining a habit of independent research is essential. Instead of using AI as a primary source, individuals should verify its outputs by consulting academic journals, industry reports, and first-hand sources. Fact-checking AI responses against authoritative references helps preserve information literacy skills while reinforcing the importance of critical assessment.

In professional settings, organisations should implement hybrid intelligence models, where AI serves as an assistant rather than a decision-maker. By structuring workflows that require human validation and contextual refinement, professionals retain their expertise while leveraging AI for efficiency rather than delegation. Encouraging structured debate, peer review, and collaborative analysis of AI-generated insights ensures that human reasoning remains central to decision-making.

Another key approach is to train cognitive resilience through active problem-solving exercises. Disciplines that require analytical depth—such as mathematics, logic, and technical problem-solving—should be practised without AI assistance to sustain independent reasoning abilities. The habit of working through complex problems without automation reinforces mental agility, ensuring that users retain the ability to navigate challenging intellectual tasks even when AI is unavailable or incorrect.

Finally, educational systems and professional training programs must adapt to the AI-augmented intellectual environment by emphasising metacognitive skills, which involve thinking about one's thinking processes. Teaching individuals to identify when AI is helpful versus when it is a cognitive shortcut will cultivate a mindset where AI is used strategically rather than passively. Socratic questioning, and research-based learning ensures that human intellectual autonomy is preserved, even in an era where AI is ubiquitous, encouraging open-ended inquiry.

The paradox of AI-enhanced knowledge is that while it offers unprecedented access to information, it also threatens the fundamental cognitive processes that define human expertise. Striking the right balance requires intentional effort to preserve independent thought, reinforce analytical rigour, and sustain engagement with complex reasoning tasks. AI should be viewed as an amplifier of human intelligence rather than a replacement for the intellectual discipline that underpins genuine expertise.

## Chapter 4: AI for Professionals – Leveraging It Without Losing Your Edge

### AI in Law, Business, Finance, and Academia: Case Studies

The integration of AI into professional domains has transformed workflows, decision-making, and analytical capabilities. However, its effectiveness depends on how it is applied—either as an augmentation tool or as a replacement for human expertise. Examining AI's role in law, business, finance, and academia highlights both its strengths and the risks of over-reliance.

In law, AI-powered legal research tools such as Westlaw Edge and LexisNexis AI assist lawyers in case analysis and can allow rapid precedent retrieving, summarising rulings, and predicting case outcomes based on historical data. These systems enhance efficiency but also introduce risks—if lawyers over-rely on AI-generated summaries without independently reviewing full cases, legal reasoning may become superficial, overlooking nuanced interpretations that affect judicial decisions.

AI in legal contract review, such as Kira Systems, improves due diligence by identifying clauses and inconsistencies. However, it struggles with context-specific legal reasoning, which requires human judgment.

In business, AI has reshaped strategic decision-making through enhancing data-driven insights. Companies use AI for consumer behaviour analysis, supply chain optimisation, and automated risk assessment. Amazon, for example, leverages AI to predict demand fluctuations and adjust logistics, increasing operational efficiency. However, blind trust in AI-driven analytics without contextual business knowledge can lead to poor strategic choices, especially in rapidly changing market conditions where historical data may not account for emerging trends.

In finance, AI has streamlined risk management, fraud detection, and portfolio optimisation. High-frequency trading firms rely on machine learning to identify trading patterns and execute rapid transactions. AI-driven credit scoring models assess loan applicants more efficiently than traditional methods, reducing bias and improving financial inclusion. Yet, there are cases where AI-driven trading systems have exacerbated market volatility, as seen in the 2010 Flash Crash, where algorithmic trading amplified price swings without human intervention—financial professionals who fail to evaluate AI-generated investment strategies critically risk exposure to systemic errors and black-box decision-making.

In academia, AI is transforming research through automated literature reviews, citation analysis, and plagiarism detection. Tools such as Semantic Scholar and Scite help researchers identify relevant papers and assess their credibility. AI-generated summaries expedite the research process, but if scholars depend entirely on these tools without engaging deeply with the original texts, they may overlook critical arguments or misinterpret findings. The challenge is ensuring that AI serves as an accelerator for academic inquiry rather than a substitute for rigorous intellectual engagement.

# Using AI for Productivity Without Eroding Expertise

AI-driven productivity tools have optimised workflows across industries, but improper reliance on them can erode professional competence. The key to effective AI use is structured augmentation—where AI assists but does not replace core human skills.

One major risk of over-reliance is the degradation of problem-solving abilities. Professionals accustomed to AI handling routine analytical tasks may gradually lose proficiency in independent analysis. For instance, financial analysts who rely on AI to detect anomalies in financial statements might become less adept at manually identifying complex fraud patterns. Similarly, legal professionals who use AI to draft contracts without cross-checking critical clauses risk missing subtle contractual loopholes that AI does not fully understand.

A more sustainable approach involves dual-layered decision-making, where AI is used to generate preliminary insights, which are then critically evaluated by human professionals. In medicine, for example, AI-driven diagnostic tools assist radiologists by flagging potential abnormalities in medical images, but final diagnoses must still be made by specialists who integrate clinical context, patient history, and expert intuition. This model ensures that AI enhances productivity without diminishing professional expertise.

Another effective strategy is rotational AI dependence—professionals should periodically perform key tasks without AI assistance to retain their skills. In finance, for instance, investment analysts might manually build valuation models alongside AI-generated forecasts to maintain their financial modelling expertise while leveraging AI's efficiency for large-scale data analysis. In academia, researchers should occasionally conduct manual literature reviews alongside AI-assisted searches to preserve their ability to engage with primary sources critically.

# AI-Assisted Research: Enhancing Critical Thinking Instead of Replacing It

AI's ability to process vast amounts of data makes it an invaluable research tool, but it must be designed to stimulate rather than suppress critical thinking. When AI is treated as an authoritative source rather than a probabilistic assistant, users risk developing a passive intellectual approach, accepting AI-generated findings without deeper inquiry.

The key to AI-assisted research is contextual verification. AI models generate summaries based on statistical relevance rather than interpretative reasoning, which means that researchers must validate outputs against original sources. AI-generated literature reviews should serve as a starting point, guiding scholars toward key papers but not replacing direct engagement with those texts.

In technical fields, AI must be paired with hypothesis-driven research methodologies. Instead of passively extracting AI-generated insights, researchers should use AI to test existing theories, compare alternative perspectives, and identify knowledge gaps. This approach transforms AI from an information retrieval tool into an intellectual amplifier, strengthening analytical depth rather than encouraging surface-level understanding.

Interdisciplinary integration also plays a crucial role in ensuring AI enhances rather than replaces intellectual inquiry. AI models trained in a single discipline may reinforce narrow perspectives, limiting their ability to generate holistic insights. Encouraging researchers to engage with AI through cross-domain queries—for example, applying economic forecasting models to environmental science—ensures that AI facilitates knowledge expansion rather than merely streamlining familiar workflows.

Finally, fostering a culture of AI scepticism ensures that professionals remain active thinkers rather than passive consumers of AI-generated content. Encouraging professionals to challenge AI outputs, identify inconsistencies, and seek alternative explanations cultivates intellectual resilience. AI should be seen as a partner in critical inquiry, not as an entity that dictates conclusions.

Therefore, we need to structure AI interactions in ways that reinforce analytical reasoning, independent validation, and interdisciplinary synthesis. Professionals can leverage AI's capabilities without compromising their expertise. The goal is to ensure that AI serves as a force multiplier for human intelligence rather than a crutch that diminishes professional skill over time.

## Chapter 5: AI for Learning – How to Train Smarter, Not Lazier

### AI-Powered Learning: Structuring Your Study Without Becoming Dependent

The integration of AI into education has created unique opportunities for personalised learning, but it also introduces the risk of passive knowledge acquisition. AI-powered tools such as adaptive tutoring systems, automated summarisation, and intelligent question generation can enhance efficiency, but if learners rely on them excessively, they may bypass the critical processes necessary for deep understanding. The challenge is to use AI as a facilitator rather than a substitute for cognitive effort, ensuring that learning remains an active rather than a passive process.

One of the primary risks of AI-assisted learning is over-reliance on pre-generated content. When students use AI to summarise textbooks, generate essays, or solve problems without engaging in the underlying logic, they absorb knowledge superficially rather than internalising it. This effect is particularly concerning in fields requiring problem-solving and critical reasoning, such as mathematics, programming, and legal analysis. If AI handles all the cognitive work, learners may develop a dependency, weakening their ability to think independently when AI is unavailable.

Students must structure their study approach in a way that maintains active engagement to counteract this. One effective strategy is the AI-assisted Socratic method, where learners use AI-generated content as a starting point but then critically evaluate, expand, or challenge it. Instead of merely reading AI summaries, students should verify key points against source material, generate their own counterarguments, and reconstruct explanations in their own words. This ensures that AI supports deeper comprehension rather than replacing the effort required for true learning.

## Designing AI-Assisted Practice Tests That Actually Improve Skills

AI-generated quizzes and practice tests have become a common feature of educational platforms, but their effectiveness depends on how they are structured. A poorly designed AI-driven assessment may reinforce pattern recognition rather than genuine understanding, leading to a superficial familiarity with concepts rather than mastery. When AI creates questions based solely on linguistic probability rather than conceptual depth, learners may unknowingly train themselves to recognise recurring phrasing instead of engaging with the underlying principles of the subject matter.

For AI-assisted testing to be genuinely beneficial, questions must be designed to promote active recall and deep processing. Traditional multiple-choice formats generated by AI can be effective for factual retention but are insufficient for developing higher-order thinking skills. Instead, learners should use AI to generate application-based, scenario-driven, or open-ended questions that require synthesis and reasoning. For instance, in finance, instead of relying on AI to produce basic definitional questions, a more effective approach would involve AI-generated case studies requiring students to apply financial models to real-world market conditions.

Another critical factor is adaptive difficulty adjustment. Many AI-based learning tools adjust question difficulty based on user performance, but blind automation of this process can create an illusion of progress. If AI lowers difficulty after incorrect responses rather than reinforcing core concepts, students may develop false confidence without addressing fundamental weaknesses. The best AI-assisted practice tests should challenge learners just beyond their comfort zone, ensuring that repeated exposure strengthens true problem-solving abilities rather than just response familiarity.

## Retaining Knowledge When AI Is Doing Most of the Work

As AI increasingly handles research, summarisation, and content generation, the risk of knowledge atrophy becomes a serious concern. When learners continuously rely on AI to perform cognitive tasks, retention decreases because the brain is not actively processing the material. Research in cognitive science suggests that active engagement—such as writing, discussing, and problem-solving—is essential for encoding information into long-term memory. AI, when used improperly, can encourage passive learning, where information is consumed but not mentally reinforced.

Learners must engage in retrieval practice, forcing their brains to recall and reconstruct information without direct AI assistance to retain knowledge effectively. One approach is the delayed recall method, where students use AI to generate explanations but then attempt to reproduce the information from memory hours or days later. This process strengthens retention and prevents over-dependence on AI-generated content.

Another effective technique is human-AI collaborative note-taking. Instead of passively accepting AI-generated summaries, students should create their own annotated versions, adding personal insights, connections, and supplementary details. AI can structure and refine these notes, but the act of manually engaging with the content ensures stronger retention.

Additionally, incorporating interleaved learning techniques—where different topics are studied in a mixed sequence—can prevent the type of shallow memorisation that AI summarisation often promotes. Instead of reviewing AI-generated content in isolation, learners should integrate AI-assisted material with traditional study methods, such as problem-solving, discussion-based learning, and hands-on applications. It ensures that knowledge is reinforced through multiple cognitive pathways rather than relying solely on AI-generated reinforcement.

Ultimately, AI is a powerful tool for optimising learning, but it must be used strategically. The most effective approach involves treating AI as a scaffold rather than a crutch, ensuring that its capabilities are harnessed to enhance comprehension, critical thinking, and long-term retention rather than diminishing the intellectual effort required for true mastery.

## Chapter 6: Ethical AI – Who Controls the Ship?

### Avoiding AI Bias and Manipulation

AI models are not neutral. They reflect the biases present in their training data and the assumptions embedded in their design. Since AI generates responses based on statistical probabilities rather than critical reasoning, it can unintentionally reinforce existing prejudices, misinformation, or ideological distortions. Bias in AI can emerge from multiple sources, including imbalanced training datasets, biased human input, and algorithmic optimisation that prioritises engagement over accuracy.

A primary concern is the self-reinforcing nature of AI-driven biases. If a model is trained on predominantly Western perspectives, for example, it may produce outputs that marginalise alternative viewpoints. Similarly, if financial AI models are disproportionately trained on historical data reflecting economic downturns, they may develop a pessimistic bias in risk assessment, leading to overly conservative investment recommendations. These issues are exacerbated when AI-generated content influences real-world decisions, reinforcing the very biases it was trained on.

Avoiding AI bias requires active intervention at multiple levels. First, developers must ensure that training data is representative, diverse, and regularly updated to mitigate historical distortions. Second, users must critically assess AI outputs rather than accepting them at face value. Blind trust in AI-generated content increases the risk of algorithmic manipulation, where biased outputs influence public perception, policymaking, or financial decisions. The responsibility for ethical AI use does not lie solely with developers—it extends to all users, who must cultivate a habit of cross-referencing AI-generated insights against independent sources.

## Understanding the Economics Behind AI Decision-Making

AI systems do not operate in a vacuum—they are shaped by economic incentives that drive their development and deployment. Large-scale AI models are not built for altruistic purposes; they exist within a commercial framework where profit motives influence design choices. Understanding the financial mechanics behind AI decision-making is crucial to recognising potential conflicts of interest in how these systems function.

One major economic factor is the monetisation of AI models. Free-tier AI tools often prioritise engagement over accuracy, optimising responses to increase user interaction rather than provide the most reliable information. In social media and content recommendation algorithms, AI is designed to maximise retention, leading to clickbait-driven outputs and sensationalism. It raises ethical concerns, as AI-driven platforms may subtly shape user behaviour, promoting content that aligns with their economic interests rather than objective truth.

In the corporate sector, AI is increasingly used for automated decision-making in hiring, loan approvals, and financial risk assessment. While these applications improve efficiency, they also introduce economic biases. AI models trained on historical hiring data, for instance, may inherit discriminatory patterns, favouring certain demographics while disadvantaging others. Similarly, financial AI models used for credit scoring might disproportionately penalise individuals from underrepresented economic backgrounds if their data is underrepresented in training datasets.

Economic incentives also influence data privacy and surveillance. Many AI models rely on user-generated data for continuous improvement, leading to concerns about data commodification and exploitation. Large technology firms use AI-driven analytics to extract consumer insights, predict purchasing behaviour, and tailor advertising strategies, raising ethical questions about consent and transparency. Users must be aware that AI is not an independent entity—it is a product shaped by financial objectives that may not always align with individual or societal well-being.

## Taking Charge of AI Instead of Being Controlled by It

The increasing integration of AI into professional and personal life creates a critical question: Who is in control—humans or AI? While AI can enhance decision-making, it must remain a tool under human oversight rather than an autonomous authority dictating choices. The risk of delegating too much decision-making power to AI is that it shifts accountability away from human judgment, creating scenarios where flawed AI outputs go unchallenged.

One of the most significant dangers is automation complacency, where users become overly reliant on AI-generated insights and gradually lose the ability to question them. This phenomenon is evident in fields such as finance, where traders use AI-driven models for portfolio management, and medicine, where AI assists in diagnostics. If professionals defer entirely to AI without applying critical scrutiny, they risk accepting mechanically generated errors as fact, leading to faulty decisions with real-world consequences.

Taking charge of AI requires active human intervention at every stage of interaction. Users must adopt a hybrid intelligence model, where AI serves as a cognitive assistant rather than an autonomous decision-maker. It refers to:

1. **Validating AI outputs through independent verification**—Cross-checking AI-generated data against external sources ensures accuracy.

2. **Interrogating AI recommendations**—Instead of accepting AI-generated conclusions, users should **probe the rationale behind outputs**, identifying any inconsistencies or potential biases.

3. **Developing AI literacy**—Understanding how AI models function helps users anticipate **systemic weaknesses** and use AI more strategically.

The long-term goal should be to integrate AI into workflows without surrendering control to it. AI should be leveraged to amplify human expertise, providing computational power while leaving final judgment and ethical responsibility in human hands.

Ethical AI use is not about resisting technological advancement—it is about ensuring that AI remains a servant to human intelligence rather than a substitute for it.

## Chapter 7: Future-Proofing Yourself – The Skills That Won't Be Automated

### What AI Can't Replace: Developing Irreplaceable Expertise

Despite the sudden AI deployment, certain human capabilities remain beyond its reach. AI excels at pattern recognition, data processing, and automation, but it lacks true creativity, emotional intelligence, and complex decision-making grounded in human experience. These irreplaceable skills form the foundation of expertise that AI cannot replicate.

One key limitation of AI is its inability to exercise independent judgment in ambiguous or novel situations. AI operates within the constraints of its training data, meaning it struggles when confronted with unstructured problems that require contextual intuition. Professions that depend on ethical reasoning, negotiation, and deep contextual awareness—such as diplomacy, leadership, and high-stakes legal advocacy—will always require human oversight. Even in data-driven fields like finance and medicine, final decision-making must remain in human hands, as AI cannot fully account for ethical implications, unforeseen variables, or the psychological dimensions of human behaviour.

Another domain where AI falls short is original thought and innovation. While generative AI can produce variations of existing ideas, it does not engage in true ideation, lateral thinking, or disruptive innovation. The most valuable professionals will be those who develop intellectual agility—the ability to synthesise ideas from multiple sources, challenge prevailing assumptions, and pioneer new solutions. The ability to frame the right questions will become as critical as answering them, as AI can generate responses but cannot define complex, high-value problems in novel ways.

## The Importance of Multidisciplinary Thinking

As AI automates routine analytical tasks, professionals must expand their expertise beyond single-domain specialisation. Multidisciplinary thinking—the ability to draw connections across different fields—will be a defining trait of those who thrive in an AI-dominated world. Since AI models are inherently compartmentalised lacking cross-domain cognitive flexibility, human professionals who can integrate knowledge across disciplines will maintain a distinct advantage.

For example, in finance, AI can optimise trading strategies through historical data analysis, but integrating knowledge of political risk, behavioural psychology, and macroeconomic trends allows a human analyst to anticipate black swan events that AI might overlook. In engineering, AI can suggest optimised designs, but an engineer who understands environmental science, supply chain logistics, and regulatory frameworks will produce solutions that align with broader economic and societal needs. The future workforce will require professionals who do not just understand one field deeply but can bridge multiple disciplines, translating insights across domains.

Multidisciplinarity also enhances AI oversight and bias detection. AI models tend to overfit to domain-specific heuristics, meaning they may fail to consider external constraints or unintended consequences. A professional with cross-disciplinary knowledge can identify where AI-driven decisions lack perspective and intervene to ensure holistic, well-balanced outcomes. The more complex and interconnected the world becomes the greater the need for professionals who can synthesise diverse knowledge streams into actionable intelligence.

## How to Position Yourself as a High-Value Professional in an AI-Dominated World

To remain competitive in an AI-driven economy, professionals must adopt a strategic approach to skill development. The most valuable individuals will be those who combine deep expertise in their domain with adaptability, problem-solving abilities, and AI fluency.

First, professionals must focus on cognitive skills that AI cannot replicate, such as critical thinking, ethical judgment, and strategic foresight. In industries where automation is rapidly replacing repetitive tasks, professionals should shift their focus from execution to oversight, quality control, and high-level decision-making. Instead of competing with AI in computational efficiency, they should develop strengths in sense-making, contextual reasoning, and leadership—areas where human cognition remains unmatched.

Second, developing AI literacy is essential. Professionals who understand how AI models operate, their limitations, and their biases will have a decisive advantage. It does not mean that every professional needs to become a programmer, but understanding the mechanics of AI decision-making, data biases, and model constraints will allow individuals to use AI as a strategic amplifier rather than a passive tool. Those who can audit, refine, and challenge AI-generated outputs will become indispensable in ensuring AI-driven processes remain accurate and aligned with business objectives.

Finally, professionals must continuously evolve their skill sets. AI does not replace entire professions—it reshapes them, automating some aspects while amplifying others. The most successful individuals will be those who anticipate industry shifts, acquire new competencies, and remain intellectually agile. Continuous learning, professional networking, and staying informed about technological trends will differentiate those who lead from those who become obsolete.

Future-proofing against automation does not mean resisting AI but positioning oneself as an expert in areas where human intelligence remains indispensable. The most valuable professionals will be those who use AI strategically, leveraging its strengths while reinforcing uniquely human capabilities that machines cannot replicate.

# Conclusion: Becoming an AI-Enhanced Thinker, Not a Follower

## Final Framework for Maintaining Control

The current integration of AI into professional and intellectual spheres presents both opportunities and risks. Those who understand its limitations, biases, and potential pitfalls can harness AI as a tool for augmentation rather than as a substitute for thinking. The key to maintaining control lies in adopting a structured framework that ensures human oversight, strategic use, and continuous skill refinement.

The first principle is critical engagement. AI outputs must never be accepted uncritically—every AI-generated response should be examined, questioned, and validated against independent sources. AI is a probabilistic model that predicts text rather than comprehending truth, making it essential to apply epistemic vigilance when using its outputs. Whether in research, decision-making, or strategic planning, users must remain the final authority, assessing whether AI-generated information aligns with real-world knowledge.

Another core element of control is intentional interaction. AI should not dictate workflows but instead be leveraged in a structured manner. Professionals who allow AI to shape their thought processes, problem-framing, and intellectual curiosity risk becoming passive consumers rather than active decision-makers. The best approach is to use AI to amplify existing expertise, prompting it to test hypotheses, refine arguments, or explore alternative perspectives—rather than simply asking it to provide pre-packaged conclusions.

A third pillar is strategic AI literacy. Understanding how AI models function, their economic incentives and their inherent biases allow users to anticipate when AI outputs may be skewed, unreliable, or incomplete. Those who possess technical fluency in AI mechanics—even at a conceptual level—are better positioned to use AI effectively without being misled by its outputs. It ensures that AI remains a servant to human intelligence, not a master that dictates conclusions.

## How to Build a System That Keeps AI as Your Assistant, Not Your Master

Users must structure interactions around human-led processes with AI augmentation to ensure that AI serves as an assistant rather than an authoritative decision-maker. The most effective approach refers to establishing decision hierarchies, where AI-generated insights are treated as input rather than final judgment.

One method is AI-assisted problem-solving, where users first formulate hypotheses or draft initial solutions independently before using AI to test, refine, or enhance their thinking. For example, in legal analysis, AI can be used to identify precedents or generate contract clauses, but the final interpretation should remain with the human expert who understands context, intent, and legal strategy.

Another key strategy is modular AI integration, where AI is incorporated into specific components of workflows without dominating the entire process. In financial analysis, AI can streamline quantitative modelling and trend analysis, but strategic investment decisions must factor in real-world market conditions, regulatory changes, and geopolitical risks—elements AI cannot fully comprehend. Similarly, in research, AI can automate literature reviews and summarisation, but critical synthesis and conceptual framework development should remain in human hands.

A third element is continuous learning and recalibration. AI models evolve, and their accuracy depends on their training data. Regular reassessment of AI tools, their reliability, and their alignment with real-world outcomes ensures that users are not passively following outdated or biased AI-generated insights. Those who periodically cross-check AI outputs with domain expertise, independent research, and professional intuition are better equipped to navigate an AI-driven world without becoming over-reliant on automated reasoning.

## Actionable Steps to Future-Proof Your Knowledge and Expertise

Individuals must continuously refine their knowledge, develop complementary skills, and strategically interact with AI to maintain intellectual independence in an AI-dominated context. The first step is to cultivate deep expertise in a core domain, ensuring that AI acts as a tool for enhancing decision-making rather than replacing domain knowledge. It is important staying updated with emerging research, industry trends, and practical applications that AI may not yet fully capture.

Another critical step is building cross-disciplinary fluency. AI excels at processing data within structured domains, but real-world complexity requires integrating insights from multiple fields. Professionals who develop interdisciplinary thinking—blending technical knowledge with fields such as psychology, ethics, and systems thinking—will have a distinct advantage over those who rely solely on AI-generated outputs.

Developing AI literacy and oversight skills is equally important, including understanding how AI models generate responses, where they introduce bias, and how to evaluate their outputs critically. Those who master AI auditing, prompt engineering, and bias detection will remain indispensable as human safeguards in AI-assisted environments.

Finally, individuals should adopt a learning model that prioritises adaptability. In a world where AI capabilities are rapidly evolving, professionals who maintain intellectual agility, embrace continuous learning, and remain proactive in updating their skill sets will be the most resilient. AI should be seen as an accelerator of human intelligence, not a replacement for it. Those who shape AI strategically—rather than allowing it to shape them—will lead in an era where technology and human expertise must coexist.

www.ingramcontent.com/pod-product-compliance
Lightning Source LLC
LaVergne TN
LVHW052313060326
832902LV00021B/3855